C

HOW TO GROW STUFF

HOW TO GROW STUFF

ALICE VINCENT

EBURY
PRESS

10 9 8 7 6 5 4 3 2 1

Ebury Press, an imprint of Ebury Publishing,
20 Vauxhall Bridge Road,
London SW1V 2SA

Ebury Press is part of the Penguin Random House group
of companies whose addresses can be found at
global.penguinrandomhouse.com

Penguin
Random House
UK

First published by Ebury Press in 2017
www.penguin.co.uk

A CIP catalogue record for this book is available from
the British Library

ISBN 9781785035593

Colour origination by Altaimage Ltd, London
Printed and bound in China by Toppan Leefung

MIX
Paper from
responsible sources
FSC® C018179
www.fsc.org

Penguin Random House is committed to a sustainable future
for our business, our readers and our planet. This book is
made from Forest Stewardship Council® certified paper.

CONTENTS

INTRODUCTION

Even my parents thought I was uncool when I told them I was going to start writing about gardening. The word conjures notions of padded foam kneelers and rose pruning – two things I remain fairly ambivalent about. But growing stuff? Now growing stuff is something most people can get into – whether cultivating your own herbs or vegetables to put on your plate or just nurturing a plant on your desk to brighten up the place.

I've been growing stuff for a couple of years now. I'm not an expert by any stretch of the imagination, but I know how to keep some things alive and how they can improve my day.

Mostly, I've taught myself, learning through mistakes and experience. I've accidentally killed things along the way, such as the herbs that were feasted on by slugs (massive, orange London slugs that even devour the lavender they're purported to hate), I've watered flowers so much that they've sprouted mushrooms, and I've planted seeds that have only grown shoots several months later – in some other plant's pot.

But I've also eaten salad straight from the plant that sits on my balcony table, grown herbs from seed that lasted all winter and encouraged flowers to bloom like clockwork all summer.

Growing things might seem difficult if you're looking at a cottage garden bursting with blooms for inspiration, but if you have smaller aspirations and just want to keep some basil alive, it's really not that hard. Better than that: it can be really satisfying, often tasty, and nearly always a little bit magical.

For three years I've made four-square metres of concrete my playground, laboratory and, eventually, a garden of sorts. My balcony is north-facing, windswept and situated on top of a hill in London – not the best conditions for growing – and yet plants have grown here, and beautifully. I have learned not to take soil for granted, and I have discovered the tiny, splendid triumph of seeing bees dine on daisies four storeys up.

You might have a window ledge, or perhaps a dauntingly overgrown back garden, but most likely you'll have something in between and something that needs of a bit of love. Maybe you want to grow stuff that looks pretty, or to eat – or both. You might not even know what you want to grow yet, or even why, and that's ok too.

Somewhere down the line, gardening became about rules: about the right kind of soil to use or how many different-coloured plants you should put in one place without it looking garish. It can get really daunting. But gardening doesn't have to be so overwhelming. Mostly, you just need a bit of gumption, an open mind and the optimism to try again if it doesn't work out.

This isn't a book to help you build a water feature or choose the right plants for a rockery. You won't learn about acidic soil or hedge clipping here – there are lots of other places where you can find out about that. This book is about growing things: herbs, vegetables, houseplants, flowers and bulbs – and with these, hopefully, your confidence. Once you've got that sorted, then we can get onto the bigger stuff.

UNIVERSAL GROWING INFO

DRAINAGE

While I have managed to grow lots of plants in containers that have very little material added to improve drainage, all plants prefer pots that let excess water drain away and stop their roots from rotting. So if you're growing in pots, it's worth adding some stones, rubble or old bits of terracotta plant pot (known as 'crocks') in the bottom of them before you fill up with compost or potting soil, which will help the drainage.
If you want to use an ornamental pot that doesn't have any holes in the bottom, you can always plant into a plastic everyday flowerpot that does have holes inside it and hide this within your pretty container. If you are using quirky, unconventional containers to grow in, such as oil cans, get out the drill and make a few holes in the base.

LIGHT AND WARMTH IS IMPORTANT

Whether your first seedlings are just popping up, or you're trying to make something from the garden centre bloom, all of the plants in this book like sunlight. So make room for them on bright windowsills and look for the sunny spots in your garden that they can make their home.

WATERING

Many beginner gardeners will overwater plants out of love and concern, causing them to wilt (which can inspire more zealous watering) and die. If you're unsure whether to water, stick a finger in the soil to check. If it feels damp, you don't need to water. If it feels dry or dusty, you do.

GROWING FROM CUTTINGS

Some plants are propagated – or reproduced – better from cuttings, rather than by sowing seeds. This means a section of a larger (parent) plant is cut off and put into a pot where it is encouraged to grow roots so it can become an entirely new plant.

If you're gardening on a budget, using cuttings from other plants – and other people's plants! – is a really good way to fill up your garden cheaply. This might seem daunting, but really it just takes a little time and the right set-up.

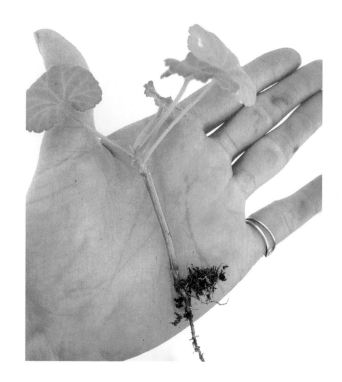

WHEN YOUR SEEDLINGS GROW

The first two leaves that appear on your seedlings will be very exciting, but these are just the plant's trainer wheels. It's the next pair of leaves, known as 'true leaves', that indicate how far the plant is growing.

If you have lots of seedlings, you can guarantee the success of the best ones by getting rid of the smaller or weaker ones around them. This is called 'thinning out'. It can feel a bit like infanticide, but it is just encouraging a natural process. If you try to make all of the seeds you've planted grow in a small space, the whole crop could suffer and not grow as well as they could, so it's better to lose a few spindly seedlings to give the healthier-looking ones the best chance in life.

RE-POTTING PLANTS

Whether you've bought an established plant or you are 'potting on' your seedlings (putting them into a bigger pot as they grow), the rules are the same: water the plants before they go in and make a big enough hole in the soil for the plant, its roots and the soil around its roots to fit in.

To remove a plant from its pot, turn it upside down so that the top of the soil and the base of the main stem is resting in your palm, then ease it out of the pot, gently loosen its roots a little, then put it into its new hole. Add soil all around the plant until it is level with the surface of the soil from the old pot, and pat or 'firm down'. Then water again.

COMPOST, FOOD AND SOIL

The minute you delve into compost, soil and fertiliser as a growing novice, things can get really daunting. There are about a million types of all of these available. When you really know your stuff, you can get picky about what you choose, but, like coffee and wine, until you become an expert, the basics will get the job done just fine.

I'd recommend using standard, good-quality potting compost to start off any of the plants in this book — you can mix in some more nutritious compost such as John Innes No 3 if you're feeling fancy. You can also add slow-release food pellets to your soil if you are growing in pots and are worried about the plants getting enough nutrients, but most plants will manage all right without. There are certain plants that will benefit from a few added extras as they start to produce fruits or flowers, but more on that later.

If you don't have a car or live in an urban area, you might want to think about buying your compost or soil online and getting it delivered.

THINK ABOUT YOUR SPACE

Gardening books and pictures online will show beautiful troughs overflowing with flowers and foliage; this idyllic picture is possible to achieve with some varieties and some containers, but if you're growing vegetables or herbs, expect a more gappy look, as they will need room to spread out and do their thing – namely, making delicious food for you.

So, take a good, hard look at your growing space and be realistic about what you can get in there. If you've only got a balcony, you'll need to get large containers to grow vegetables. (Make sure your balcony can handle the weight.)

If you have only a windowsill, look out for dwarf varieties of plants. Even if you have a great big garden – you lucky thing – pay attention to which are the sunny and shady bits, and where space can be freed up that is best for what you want to grow.

PESTS AND PROBLEMS

Depending on the kind of space you're gardening in, you're going to encounter pests and your plants may be prone to common problems.

Slugs aren't particularly fussy – in certain gardens they will devour almost anything. But they can be easily defeated by organic slug

pellets. Scatter these around the base of your growing plants according to packet instructions. A cheaper method is to do the same thing with broken egg shells and or coffee grinds.

Greenfly or aphids have a soft spot for the delicious new foliage and flowerbuds of plants such as pansies, but I've also found them on sprouting bulbs and vegetable leaves. I prefer to use a general-use bug killer, but other gardeners swear by a persistent habit of spraying jets of water onto the insects. You can also mix some washing-up liquid or liquid soap in a spray bottle, although this isn't quite as effective.

Some insects make a plant less pretty but don't do any lasting damage. Flea beetles like to make tiny holes in rocket leaves. These are totally harmless, although the results might not win you any prizes. If it really bothers you, loosely cover your crop in landscaping fabric and hold it down with stones or stakes. This will let in the light, air and water, but stop any bugs getting to your crop.

Most plants will be more prone to developing diseases if they are not properly fed and watered. Powdery mildew is a common problem, which courgettes and tomatoes are susceptible to, which sees the plant's leaves and stems become covered in a light white or grey dust. It spreads very easily and there are no fungicides available for edible plants. The best cure, therefore, is to keep your courgettes well-watered and to remove any affected leaves as soon as you see them by cutting them off.

Often a disease won't mean the death of the whole plant if you take steps to stop it before it gets too advanced. Looking carefully at your courgettes and tomatoes will help you stop diseases from getting worse.

If your tomatoes develop blackened patches where the stem meets the fruit, this is probably blossom end rot and is caused by the soil not being consistently moist. Remove the affected fruit and make sure that you are watering regularly.

Both courgettes and tomatoes will be best set against ailments if they are regularly fed and watered. Set a reminder to feed and water consistently, if that helps, remove any yellow leaves as they appear and make sure the plants aren't given too much hot sunshine.

KEEP AN EYE ON STUFF

Growing becomes addictively rewarding when you start paying a little attention. Before you know it, you'll be rushing out to tend your plants the minute you get back from work or a holiday. Try to take a look at your lot every day to see how things are doing – this, more than anything, is the best way to learn about your plants and what they need to grow well.

GROW TABLE

X = plant now outside

Y = plant now inside

	Anytime	Jan	Feb	Mar	Apr	May
Aloe Vera	X					
Basil				Y	Y	X
Chillies		Y	Y	Y	Y	
Courgettes				Y	Y	X
Daffodils			X	X		
Geraniums				X	X	X
Hyacinths		Y	Y	X	X	
Lavender				X	X	X
Maidenhair fern	Y					
Mint				X	X	X
Money Plant	Y					
Muscari			X	X	X	
Osteospermum					X	X
Oxalis	Y					
Pansies		XY	XY	X	X	
Parsley			Y	Y	XY	XY
Rocket	X					
Rosemary	XY					
Tomatoes			Y	Y	X	X
Tulips					X	X

Jun	Jul	Aug	Sep	Oct	Nov	Dec
X	X	X				
X	X					
			X	X		
X	X	X	X			
			XY	XY	Y	Y
X	X	XY	Y			
X	X	X				
		XY	XY	XY		
X	X					
	X	X	X	X	X	X
XY	XY	XY	XY			
X	X	X				
				X	X	

1
HERBS

If you've never grown anything before, herbs are the best place to start. They are cheap, unthreatening and a pot or packet of seeds can be picked up in a supermarket aisle.

It's easy to be taken in by the delightful-looking wooden planters filled with lots of different types of herbs, but it can be tricky to keep them all looking lovely if you're just starting out. Basil, for instance, needs far less water than parsley, while mint and rosemary both like their space. Shoving them all together in one vintage wine crate can be the equivalent of a botanical Big Brother house – they're unlikely to all get along nicely.

So, this chapter will teach you how to grow and look after four useful, everyday herbs that look, smell and taste wonderful. Basil, mint and parsley elevate countless salads, sauces and cocktails, while rosemary adds as much depth and substance to heartier meals as it will your outside space.

Plus, all of them flower beautifully, attracting bees and other wildlife to your home. So if you do grow more parsley than you can eat, let it flower and you know that another creature is benefitting from your endeavours.

HOW LONG WILL MY HERB PLANTS LAST?

While rosemary can live for years in the right conditions, basil, mint and parsley are all treated here as one-season plants, or annuals. Although parsley and mint can return for another spring, it's better to enjoy your herbs while they are in their prime and to encourage them to keep cropping during their growing seasons, so consider any extra subsequent growth a bonus.

THE BEST WAY TO PICK HERBS

To keep your herbs bushy and beautiful, only take leaves from the top of the plant when you are picking them. Look out for the tiny new leaf nodules growing lower down on the stems and cut or pinch off the stem and leaves that grow above them. This is called 'pinching out' and it will encourage new growth outwards, rather than upwards.

If you just pick leaves from the side of the stems, you'll end up with a plant that has long, bare, woody stalks and fewer leaves.

GETTING YOUR HERBS TO MAKE LEAVES, NOT FLOWERS

When parsley, basil and mint are exposed to hotter temperatures they can 'bolt'. This means the plant grows very tall very quickly and produces flowers to try to make seeds so it can reproduce before it dies.

While this looks impressive, it isn't great for the quality of your herbs, as the plant is putting energy into making seeds rather than delicious leaves. So, pinch off those little flowers along with two sets of leaves underneath. If there's enough of a stem, pop them in a glass of water – they smell great.

BASIL

The first plant I nurtured as a pretend grown up. If you want to make this your foray into herb growing, it's not a bad way to start. You can pick up a basil plant cheaply from the supermarket any time of year.

I've grown a few varieties – purple, lettuce, sweet – with mixed success, and I now generally accept that it's a herb to cherish while it lives and should be replaced when it goes past its best.

Basil hails from India and now grows in Mediterranean countries, so it likes sunshine and warmth.

HOW TO GROW

Take off the plastic wrap around the plant and pop the whole thing, including the pot, on a saucer or in a fancier container. Keep inside, somewhere warm and sunny – a windowsill will do – and let its leaves gloriously flop out.

Supermarket herbs are usually very well watered, so there's no need to water it unless the soil is dry. Leave it be for a few days to settle into its new home. Basil never needs watering as much as people think it does; the trick is to wait until the soil is dry and the plant looks on the verge of wilting, then give it enough water that it just starts to run out into the saucer or pot.

If you have forgotten to water it and the plant doesn't recover after a thorough soaking, accept defeat and pick all the leaves. They can be chopped up and frozen, or made into pesto. Go and buy a new plant.

Make sure you turn your basil around in the light every few days to encourage growth on all sides.

If you've managed to keep your basil alive, you may want to treat it to a summer holiday outside. Warm weather can encourage more vigorous growth. Decant the plant into a bigger pot with stones at the bottom (for drainage) and topped with compost or into a hole in a flowerbed. Either water the basil before it goes in, or give it a soaking once you've put it in the new soil and patted it down. After a few days, water it regularly if it's warm and sunny outside, and less when it's cooler.

When the weather gets colder later in the year, take your basil back inside. If it's looking peaky, you might be better off digging it out and composting it to let the ground rest over winter, or to make space so you can plant something else.

GROWING FROM SEED

Basil can be grown from seed but this requires more patience.

Put about 8–10 seeds in one flowerpot that is roughly the size of your palm. Cover them with a thin layer of soil. Give the pot a light watering so that the soil feels damp but not wet. Unless it's summer, keep your pot inside on a sunny windowsill. Otherwise, put the pot outside in a sunny spot and water every few days. Tiny shoots should appear after

about 10 days, followed by flat semi-circular leaves in two or three weeks — these are the baby basil's starter leaves (see page 15).

Once the baby basils are between 5 and 10cm tall and have at least two sets of true leaves you can transport them to bigger pots or the ground outside. Give them enough room to grow: basil can get pretty big in the right conditions, so plant your seedlings about 15cm apart.

Although some basil plants will die back and reappear the next year (gardeners call these 'perennials'), most of them are just one-summer plants (known as 'annuals').

MINT

When it comes to mint, the first thing that experienced gardeners will try to bamboozle you with are the different varieties available – there are loads of them. The vast majority are very easy to grow and can be quite bossy (or invasive) in your garden, and will take over the space of other plants.

You might want to start with growing either sweet mint or spearmint. Sweet mint has large, bright green leaves and a pleasant, all-round taste and is good for salads, cocktails, tea and general cooking. Spearmint is even more versatile and is the type that is most frequently used in cooking. Both are good for beginners and require similar care, and if you get really into gardening you can look into growing other types.

The biggest problem with mint is controlling it. If you plant it straight into the ground, prepare for a fragrant takeover – mint sends its roots out far and wide, sprouting new mini mint plants in the process, which is why it's best to grow it in a container. If it's in a pot, you can keep it indoors, too.

HOW TO GROW

Mint is best bought as a baby plant in spring; it should last you all the way through to the winter, before dying back and returning the next year. Like basil and parsley, you can start growing mint from a plant found in the supermarket herb aisle. If you want to grow your shop-bought mint outside, harden it off for a few days first. If you bought it at a plant nursery, it can be potted up in a container outside straight away.

Mint grows best in a container that is wider than it is deep – something shaped a bit like a salad bowl – but make sure it has holes in the bottom. Fill this up with potting mix or compost, and stick the plant in the middle. It will grow to fill the space quite quickly. Don't be tempted to plant two very different types of mint next to each other, as this can weaken their individual flavours.

Mint grows best in partial shade and likes to live in moist soil, so make sure you give it plenty of water on hot and sunny days. If you're keeping it inside, it will benefit from being misted or sprayed, as well as watered normally.

You can pick the leaves between late spring and autumn. As with other herbs, picking regularly from the top will keep your plant bushy as it will put out new stems. Over winter, your mint will probably die back, so pick all of the leaves before this happens and freeze them.

WHEN YOUR MINT GETS OLD

Mint will flower in the summer, which means you can cut those stems that have flowered down to 5cm above the soil. This will encourage nice new, tidy growth.

After a year or two, your mint plant may start to look a bit big and bedraggled. This is because it has put out loads of those long roots in the container and got tangled up with itself. This is the right time to take the plant out of its pot and look for new mint babies growing away from the main plant. You're looking for smaller plants with healthy leaves and a good base of roots. Pluck them out, sever them from their parent and plant them up in separate pots.

Alternatively, you can pull the rootball of the main plant into two, or use a spade to cut it in half, then put both sections into new containers.

GROWING FROM CUTTINGS

New mint plants are best grown from cuttings. Pretty much any sprig of mint, with leaves or otherwise, can be made to grow roots. Cut the sprig away from the plant about 1cm above the point where two other stems meet, so that the existing plant will grow more stems in its place.

Stick the cutting in a glass of water, maybe with a little soil in it to help things along, and in a week roots should appear. Keep the water level topped up, and after a few more days the roots will be long enough for the mint cutting to be potted up to grow into a new plant.

PARSLEY

Until I started growing it, I would buy parsley in enormous bunches from the greengrocers, which even the most enthusiastic herb fan wouldn't be able to thrash through. Now I grow my own, and the smell and flavour is even better when it's picked seconds before it gets added to a salad or sauce.

As far as varieties go, I prefer the flat-leaved stuff – it has a stronger flavour and is easier to grow. Parsley is generally considered a one-season plant, but I've kept one going for longer than I can remember. I've witnessed a supermarket pot of parsley thrive, die and magically revive out on the balcony, and I have also grown it from seed in a matter of weeks; it's perfect for a windowsill, too.

HOW TO GROW

If you want a cheap and easy venture into parsley growing, start off with a pot picked up from the supermarket.

Parsley likes drainage, moist soil and some sunshine. Unless its roots are sticking out of the bottom of the pot or you want to plant it straight outside, you can leave your new plant be for a while. If you are re-potting it, put some potting mix or garden soil into a container slightly larger than the one the parsley came in – make sure it has holes in the bottom to let the water out. Position it somewhere sheltered but sunny, or leave it inside on your windowsill.

Water it regularly, especially during the summer, and if you like, give it some tomato feed once a month.

In hotter temperatures, parsley will rush to put out flowerheads — otherwise known as 'bolting'. Some people actually grow parsley for the flowers alone. If you love wildlife more than eating parsley, let them grow, as they are bee-friendly. Otherwise, snip them off to encourage more vigorous leaf growth. Some people eat the young flowers in salad, too.

Flat-leaved parsley in particular will put up with cooler temperatures, but do accept that your plant might not make it through the winter. Keep one inside if you want fresh parsley in the colder months and see if your outdoor parsley revives in the spring.

HOW TO CUT PARSLEY

Parsley is naturally quite full and bushy, so unlike mint or basil it won't get 'leggy' — or tall and spindly — unless it's really deprived of sunshine. That means you harvest it slightly differently, cutting the sprigs you need from low down on the plant, a few centimetres up from where the stems meet the soil.

Keep picking your parsley to stop it getting tough. If you don't need the leaves straight away, you can freeze them in a little bit of water in ice-cube trays.

WHEN PARSLEY GETS UGLY

As the weather cools down, or if your plant gets too dry, some of the shoots will turn pale yellow and become crispy. If you ignore them, nothing bad will happen, but if you carefully snip them off at the base of the plant, that will encourage new green shoots to grow instead.

GROWING FROM SEED

Growing parsley from seed has a dodgy reputation, but that's mostly just because it takes quite a long time to germinate. I've grown it from seed for a couple of years now, and I'm really impatient, so it can be done!

Parsley seeds benefit from having good soil, room and warmth. Give yourself a fighting chance by starting them off inside any time between late winter and mid-spring, where they should germinate in a week in a warm room, rather than the three or four weeks it can take outside.

If you're really feeling keen, you can soak your seeds in warm water overnight before you plant them. This breaks through the seeds' tough outer casing and helps them germinate. In the morning, pour the whole lot through a sieve and leave them to dry on some paper.

Use a seed tray or small pots that are filled with fresh potting mix, and make sure the soil is moist. Only put a couple of seeds in each space or pot, as parsley doesn't like being overcrowded.

Keep the soil moist and when seedlings appear, water them lightly every day. If you're growing your plants on a windowsill, when they reach about 10cm tall and there's no chance of frost outside, they're ready to be moved outdoors or to a bigger pot.

Make sure there is a lot of room between each seedling. If some of them look a bit weedy or small, pull them out and throw them away. This is called 'thinning out', and it means that the strongest plants are given the best chance of survival.

Water them once a week and you'll be able to start eating your parsley once three sets of 'true leaves' have grown.

ROSEMARY

Rosemary isn't a particularly sexy herb but I love it for its hardiness, heady scent and delicate, pastel-coloured flowers, which bees adore.

This herb hails from the Mediterranean, where it thrives on dry hillsides, but it is also happy in cooler weather and manages droughts far better than being overwatered. It's evergreen, and a proven container plant, and lasts longer than the other herbs suggested here, and if you give it room to grow you've got one of the most fragrant bushes around.

HOW TO GROW

Rosemary plants can be bought in pretty much any size from flower markets or nurseries all year round. You might even find them in the herb section of your supermarket if you're lucky.

I've kept a rosemary plant happy for a couple of years in an exposed window box with no drainage, but it's worth remembering that they can suffer from root rot. Mixing in some grit or sand to your soil will help, or use a container with holes in the bottom.

Take your shop-bought rosemary out of the pot and move it into a suitable space in your flowerbed or to a larger container. The more room the plant has, the larger it will grow. Make sure that you're planting it somewhere with plenty of light – rosemary likes it sunny, and ideally with some shelter.

HOW TO HARVEST

Wait a few weeks before hacking into your rosemary for a roast dinner, and always cut your sprigs from the top of the plant, where they are softer. The tougher, woodier stems lower down will grow new leaves in their place.

Once the plant gets established, you'll have an unlimited supply of fragrant leaves, all year round, for several years. However, if you live somewhere particularly cold, your rosemary might not last as long, so be prepared to buy another plant if it doesn't look great the next spring.

KEEPING ROSEMARY HAPPY

A happy rosemary plant will have shiny green leaves, so if they change colour it's because something's not right.

If leaves turn brown and drop off, check the soil – you are probably watering it too much, causing its roots to suffocate and maybe rot. If the soil feels very damp, don't give it a drink until it has totally dried out.

Yellow leaves are a sign that the plant needs fertiliser or is 'pot bound', meaning the roots need more room. If the plant is in a pot, check to see if roots are coming out of the holes in the bottom. If so, move it into a bigger home. If it has plenty of room, give it a little tomato feed.

CUTTING BACK ROSEMARY

You can snip off bits of rosemary for cooking or decoration all year round, but if you want to keep the plant bushy and green year after year, you might want to give it an annual trim. This can be deeply satisfying.

Wait until mid-spring, after your rosemary has bloomed, then use scissors or secateurs (a pair of sharp scissors made for cutting through woody stems are deeply useful and worth spending on) to cut away any straggly or woody stems. When the rosemary starts growing again, it will do so with extra-tidy vigour.

The off-cuts from this trimming can be tied together, hung up and dried for cooking or used to grow a new plant.

GROWING FROM CUTTINGS

Take one of the branches of your plant and snip it just where the stem turns brown and woody, around 8–10cm down. This is your cutting.

Strip the lower leaves off the cutting and plant it in a small pot, with holes in the bottom, that is full of soil and grit, burying half of the length of the stem in the soil. Put this pot in a deep saucer or dish of water. Leave outside in a sunny place.

Check the water level doesn't get too low and leave it be. In a month or two, you should see roots appearing out of the bottom of the pot. This means the cutting has rooted and is ready to be potted on – congratulations, you've got a new rosemary plant!

2
VEG & SALAD

Despite knowing that people have been growing their own vegetables since the start of civilisation, it can still feel a bit daunting when you first get started. It brings to mind lost weekends spent thinning out carrots, allotments and zealous home-produce competitors.

But you don't have to have an interest in creating jumbo prize cabbages to grow your own food. Start small and you'll be amazed at what you'll be eating from the ground by the end of the summer.

This chapter will teach you how to grow tomatoes, chillies, courgettes and rocket – all of which can grow like weeds and if harvested all together can be turned into a pretty mean ratatouille. Have a read, take a look at the space you've got and work out which of these – if not all – you might fancy growing, then give it a go.

HOW LONG DO VEGETABLE PLANTS LAST?

All of these vegetables are 'annuals', or one-season plants. That means that you sow the seeds, they grow, put out fruit and then die back, all in the space of one season. While some people valiantly keep their chilli plants going over winter, known as 'overwintering', unless you're really attached to your plant you might have better luck starting again with a new plant the following season.

Rocket can self-seed, meaning that it can grow again the following year from the seeds it puts out at the end of its season, but generally it's best to love and lose your vegetables – and give it another shot the next year.

DO YOU HAVE ENOUGH ROOM FOR VEGETABLES?

There are plenty of people living in cities who grow vegetables. I've known courgettes be cultivated on rooftops and have eaten tomatoes straight from plants growing on my kitchen windowsill. Saying that, though, vegetables need room if they are to give you a decent crop. This might mean just having one courgette plant in a large tub rather than several, but you'll still get plenty of courgettes from just a single plant. It might also mean choosing a dwarf tomato or chilli plant instead of one of the bigger varieties.

HAND-POLLINATION

As you might remember from biology lessons, pollination happens when pollen is transferred between flowers, which results in fertilisation and, bingo, vegetables.

Many vegetables, such as onions, peas and greens, will grow quite happily from seed without any pollination assistance, but others need help from bees and other insects. When there aren't insects around to do this – for instance if you are growing plants indoors – that's when you, the trusty vegetable guardian, will have to get involved. I have known people play Marvin Gaye's 'Sexual Healing' while hand-pollinating, but that's totally optional....

You may have to hand-pollinate your chilli and courgette plants in particular to get them going, but don't worry, it's really simple (see pages 58 and 66).

FEEDING YOUR VEGETABLES

All of the vegetables I've listed here will benefit from having some organic matter – otherwise known as leaf mulch, composted manure or household compost – mixed into the soil they are being grown in. This will give the plant the nutrients it needs to really put out its best vegetables.

You can buy compost for growing vegetables online and mix it into your soil. Some growbags (a massive plastic bag for growing vegetables in which lets out water) come filled with nutrient-rich soil.

You might live in a community that generates its own compost from household waste – this stuff can be absolute gold dust, so if you can get hold of some, do, and mix it in with your soil.

It's ok if you don't mix nutrients into your soil before you grow your vegetables, but it's important to feed them while they're growing. Tomato feed will work for all of the plants in this chapter.

CHILLIES

People can get really obsessive about chilli peppers – the colour, the heat, the endless types of food they can be mixed into. If you enjoy growing them, there are dozens of seed varieties to try.

Buying seedlings or fruit-bearing plants is more cost-effective than paying 60p for a packet of three chillies from the supermarket that will sit sadly in the fridge – not to mention considerably more tasty.

The chilli originates from South America and was first domestically grown in Mexico 6,000 years ago. So technically it shouldn't really like cold, grey weather, but you can grow chilli peppers in your garden and on your windowsill provided you're prepared for the long game.

If you're not, it's still worth buying a plant and keeping it indoors – it will brighten up your home and give you the satisfaction of using ingredients picked straight from the plant.

HOW TO GROW

While it's important to keep the soil moist when chilli plants are small, when they're more established you can let them get a little drier because when these plants are stressed or struggling for water they produce hotter chillies.

You can pick up an established, fruit-bearing chilli plant from the supermarket or some nurseries and flower markets at most points during the year. A chilli plant will produce peppers between July and October, generally speaking. So if you buy a shop-bought plant in early summer, you can expect a few months' worth. If you're buying one any later, enjoy it while it lasts and accept that it may not put out any more peppers once you've picked it bare.

Once you get your plant home, have a look under its pot. If there are roots coming out of the drainage holes, it's ready to be put into a bigger pot, which will encourage it to grow bigger and put out more fruit.

Move it to a slightly bigger pot full of compost and give it a drink. If you want to grow your chillies outside, move the pot outside during the day but bring it in at night for a few days to get it acclimatised to the weather.

If your plant only has flowers on, and no fruit yet, these flowers will need to be pollinated in order to fruit. If your plant is outside, then there will be insects ready to do that for you, but if you're growing your chilli plant inside, leave a window nearby open, or be prepared to hand-pollinate. Take a cotton bud or fine paintbrush and touch the inside of each flower, transferring the pollen from one to another (see page 66).

GROWING FROM SEED

Keep them warm and cosy, and chillies can be ludicrously easy to grow from seed. I once forgot about some left in an airing cupboard for a couple of weeks only to find a dozen tiny seedlings when I went back to them.

There are lots of different types available. From a growing perspective, this largely affects the germination time – how long it will be before you'll see sprouts coming up.

If you want particularly spicy peppers for the summer, you'll need to start sowing seeds in January or February, but you can still sow in April and get some results.

Regardless of when you're sowing seeds, you'll want to do it indoors. Start off with small individual pots or a seed tray full of lightly watered compost. Lightly scatter the seeds over the soil surface and cover them with a little more compost. Slide the whole thing into a clear plastic bag, which creates a mini greenhouse, and put it somewhere warm, like an airing cupboard or a really sunny windowsill in a warm room.

In a week to ten days you should see seedlings popping up. Now you can ditch the plastic bag and move the tray to a sunny spot indoors, uncovered. Keep the soil just moist, ideally spritzing it with a water spray bottle.

When the chilli seedlings are big enough for you to handle them, carefully remove them from their starter homes by pushing a pencil underneath the roots of each seedling and, holding onto a leaf, lift them and move them into individual pots each about the size of your palm. They can be left in these for around three months – don't forget to water them, though!

When you see roots appearing at drainage holes at the bottom of the pots, it's time to move the chillies on.

If you have outdoor space, plant them into the soil, giving them plenty of room. Ideally set each plant half a metre apart, or three to a growbag. Prepare them for the great outdoors first by hardening them off for a few days (see page 58).

If you don't have that much space, chillies can be grown indoors as long as there's plenty of light and warmth. A sunny windowsill is ideal. Move one plant into a 2-litre tub (the size is stated on the pot).

Keep watering them regularly. First you'll see the flowers, then the first fruit will appear – this is when you can start giving them tomato feed once a week.

PICKING YOUR CHILLIES

With any luck, you'll have some bright red chillies on your plant before the end of summer. Use scissors, a knife or secateurs to carefully cut the pepper from its stem.

If there's been a lack of hot sunny days, the fruit may not ripen before September. This is ok, but you'll want to bring any outdoor plants inside to a warm, sunny windowsill to give the peppers a chance to ripen before you pick them.

COURGETTES

Once they get going, courgettes just don't quit. If you know someone who grows them, chances are you'll have been given at least one of their crop. These plants are so prolific that you'll only need a couple to keep you in rich courgette supply all summer – between July and October the plants can even put out a few courgettes a week, so if you're going to grow them, be prepared with a few recipe ideas to deal with that glut!

The good news is that these plants are easy to grow and have beautiful big yellow flowers (which are as delicious as the vegetables). Courgettes have both male and female flowers, which need to be pollinated in order to produce fruit. Traditionally, bees help to do this, but sometimes you might find that you need to step in (see page 66).

With a little luck, good light and a lot of water, you'll be making courgette cake by September.

HOW TO GROW

Young courgette plants can be found for sale at nurseries, flower markets and greengrocers in late spring or early summer. If you're buying these, ask the seller if the plants have been left outside – or 'hardened off' – yet. It's a simple but important step for growing vegetables outside.

Courgettes are not too fond of cold weather, and frost will kill them, so if your new plants have never really been outside overnight, you'll need to take them inside every evening for the first few days when they're in their new home.

When it gets warm outside, in early summer, and the plants are about 15–20cm tall, they can be moved into the garden. If you're planting them straight into your garden soil, think about digging some manure or compost into the ground before you do so, especially if you're growing a few types of other vegetables alongside the courgettes. Your courgettes will thank you. If you haven't prepared the soil, just make sure you feed the plants regularly.

If you're growing your courgettes in containers, your best bet is to use a growbag full of compost. Courgettes love space, so two plants per growbag or one in a large container is a good shout. Container-grown plants run out of nutrients more quickly than those in the ground, so you'll need to give them tomato feed as they grow.

As with anything that you pot on, water the plant before it moves into its new home, and water it again once you've patted it down in there, too. You will need to regularly water your plants a little when they are small and then increase the watering when they start to flower and produce fruit, and add tomato feed to that water once a week. Too much water when the plants are young can lead to rot, though, so take it easy until the plants are properly established. Remember to check the soil before watering to see how dry it is.

You can harvest your courgettes when they are only a few centimetres long or wait until they've grown to something resembling a shop-bought one, but it's important to cut them off before they get too big, otherwise you'll end up with just a few old marrows rather than dozens of lovely little courgettes.

Take a sharp knife and slice through the stem that attaches the vegetable to the plant. If you've cut off a leaf in the process, don't worry – it'll grow back.

GROWING FROM SEED

Courgettes are easy to grow from seed and it's a good way to try different varieties, or just reap the self-satisfied benefits of knowing you've brought those beauties into the world.

Because courgettes like it warm, start your seeds off in pots inside in the middle of spring. Use pots that are about as wide as your palm, and plant one seed per pot. This may sound luxurious, but courgettes need space.

You probably don't want to plant any more than four seeds in total. This allows for a couple of plants not to make it, and if they do, you can give them away.

Put compost in the pot, smooth off the top and tap the pot a couple of times on the work surface to level off the soil.

Stick your finger in the middle of the pot and pop a courgette seed in so it's standing up vertically. It's worth checking the packet instructions for the variety you've chosen, but usually seeds need to be 2.5cm beneath the soil surface.

Cover with more compost and give it some water. They should be ready to pot out in about a month, as long as there's no chance of a frost.

FLOWERS FOR FOOD AND MAKING COURGETTE BABIES

Courgette plants need to get the pollen from their male flowers inside their female flowers in order to make courgette babies. When your plants first start to flower, the ones that appear will be male flowers – at the end of a thin stem. Soon after, female courgette flowers will appear at the end of baby courgettes.

If it's a cold summer and you're not having much luck getting any fruit from your plants, you might need to pollinate the flowers yourself. So, get a cotton bud and swab the pollen from inside the male flower then gently transfer it to the stamen, or pointy middle bit, of the female flower.

Once the female flowers are pollinated, the male ones will fall off, ready for you to eat.

ROCKET

I grow a variety of salad leaves every year and once they get going, you really have to eat quite a lot of greens to keep up with them. But if I was only able to pick one, a desert-island leaf, so to speak, it would be rocket.

Granted, it's got a cool name and a killer spicy taste, but rocket is also incredibly tolerant, very easy to grow in all sorts of spaces and the difference between the sad, limp, shop-bought stuff you get in bags and that which you can freshly pick and eat is astounding.

Unlike other leaves, which involve a certain level of salad preparation, you can add freshly picked rocket to basically anything. I've picked leaves with minutes to go before I rush off to get my train in the morning and chucked them on top of some leftovers to make an instant lunch.

HOW TO GROW

You should be able to find rocket plug or starter plants in garden nurseries in late spring. Otherwise, head online. If you can't find any, don't worry, it really is very easy to grow from seed.

Rocket is native to bits of the Mediterranean such as Morocco and Turkey, where its leaves grow enormous, tough and peppery. But it actually likes being kept damp and out of too much direct sunlight – otherwise it can bolt, meaning it will put out seeds and flowers and the leaves won't have as much flavour. You can eat the seeds and flowers too, but it's better to cut them off so that the plant puts more energy into the leaves.

Be wary of watering rocket too much, as this can weaken the flavour of the leaves.

GROWING FROM SEED

You can sow rocket seed between spring and early autumn, which will give you a crop all through the summer and all winter, if you're lucky. You're most likely to keep the leaves coming if you cover the plants under some landscaping fabric or a cloche, which is like a kind of tiny moveable greenhouse.

There's no need to start these seeds off inside, in fact, rocket is less likely to bolt if you sow it in the middle of summer outside.

Whether you're growing rocket in containers or straight outside, it will thank you for using compost mixed in with your soil. If you're planting into beds, mark out shallow little valleys in the soil with your hand or a trowel and water into them. This means the seeds will go into damp soil, then cover them over with some of the nearby damp soil. Keep watering regularly, especially if it's been hot outside, and you will have leaves that are ready to eat within a month.

If you really love rocket, keep sowing seeds over the coming weeks to keep a regular crop going.

HOW TO PICK ROCKET LEAVES

You can pick the leaves when they're around 10cm long. The smaller leaves are less peppery than the big ones.

Rocket is a cut-and-come-again crop, which means you can pretty much eviscerate it and it will reward you with new leaves.

If you only want a few for a garnish, you can pick the best-looking ones, especially earlier in the season. But as time goes on and those leaves get larger, you can take a pair of scissors and cut the plant by about two-thirds. It will grow back pretty quickly, and the second leaves tend to be more spiky-edged than the first.

Even if you religiously cut off the buds and flowers that rocket puts out as it's going to seed, it will end up in bloom by the end of the season. At this point, you can cut it right back or uproot it and use the space to grow another crop.

Alternatively, if you have the space and are feeling lazy, leave it be. The plant will do as nature intended and lay seeds for next year.

TOMATOES

I first learned how tomatoes grew from my granddad. Small, shiny and green, they would tumble all over the inside of his greenhouse, filling the warm air with the peppery scent of their leaves.

Tomatoes can be really fertile and easy to grow, as long as they have light, water and a bit of room. I don't have the luxury of a greenhouse, but even so I've grown tomatoes on a windowsill that are red and sweet enough to eat, and also lured them out of compost without even meaning to, thanks to seeds grasping at life after being thrown out in a neighbour's rubbish.

Once you've tasted your own tomatoes, the bland supermarket offerings can be deeply disappointing. If you get the hang of it, you can also grow all different types and colours.

HOW TO GROW

In late spring and early summer small tomato plants can be found for sale at most nurseries and flower markets and even some local greengrocers or supermarkets. Tomato plants need to be kept moist and be fed regularly once the flowers begin to appear. Water them a little every few days and feed with tomato feed according to the packet instructions – usually once a week until the plants get established, when you only need do it every 10–14 days.

If the plants arrive together in a tray, they'll need moving into their own individual pots. Use a pencil to unearth the roots while holding onto one of the 'true' leaves (see page 15). It's really important that you don't pull the seedling out by its stem, because that can kill the plant.

If the small plants are already in individual pots, wait until they're about 15–20cm tall before you re-pot them – or 'pot them on'. Then you can put them straight into the ground in your garden, or into a growbag or container.

If you are planting into a growbag or container, leave a bit of room between the rim of it and the soil surface so you can add in more compost later if the tomato plant puts out more roots.

Your tomato plants will get very tall, so it's important to secure the stems against wooden stakes or bamboo canes as they grow. You can buy these quite cheaply from supermarkets or hardware shops, or online, then use string or twine to tie the stem to the stake to make sure they don't fall over and hurt themselves, particularly when they are heavily laden with fruit.

GETTING THE BEST TOMATOES

When you buy tomatoes on the vine from the supermarket, the green bit attached to the plant is known as the 'truss'. After these first appear on the sides of your plant, they will start putting out little yellow flowers, which will lead to your first tomatoes.

Fewer trusses will mean more ripe tomatoes, so once a plant has four or five trusses, stop the shoot from growing any more by pinching it off (literally snapping the top off with your nails) above the top truss. You want your plant to put all of its energy into making tomatoes, so gently pull off any side shoots that are appearing, too – they won't help you make your dinner.

Let your tomatoes ripen on the vine, and when they're red and plump, gently pull them off.

GROWING FROM SEED

Tomato plants are pretty easy to germinate. Start your seeds off on a windowsill indoors in early to mid-March.

Get a pot of good compost, pat it down and give it a little water. Put a few seeds on top, and cover with a thin layer of compost. Water it a little more, and keep the soil moist. Don't be tempted to drench it, though, as this can lead to disease.

You should have seedlings in a week or two. By mid-May, when risk of frost has passed, you can move them outside.

GROWING INDOORS

I've had success with some really cute small tomato plants, which
are brilliant if you only have a limited amount of space, or even just
a windowsill. Look out for plants and seeds called 'dwarf' varieties,
as these will be smaller. Then grow these according to the packet
instructions, or just sow as on the opposite page.

You can also grow tomatoes vertically if you're really short on space –
which means growing them in pots fixed to a wall or fence, or even in
hanging baskets. You can even grow them upside down! When you re-pot
your seedlings or small plant, plant them upside down through a small
hole in a bucket or hanging basket, and hang this up. Make sure you
remember to water them, though, and be prepared for some leakage!

3
FLOWERS

As lists of simple pleasures go, buying a bunch of flowers for a few quid comes near to the top. People who love flowers say that their appeal lies in their transience, knowing that they can't last forever. This is all well and good, but as someone who loves buying flowers, I can confidently say that growing them is better.

When I first started growing things, I would buy plants that were already in bloom, take them home, lovingly mistreat them and hopefully wait for flowers that would never return. When flowering plants are happy, they'll put on an absolute show, but there are some varieties that are tricky little blighters and are best left to the experts.

The first four I've included here – geraniums, lavender, osteospermum, or daisies, and pansies – are among the most lovable and reliable flowers around. All of them look delightful, come in a variety of colours and will put up with your well-intentioned rookie errors. Lavender smells like a dream, too.

Together, these four will give you flowers all year round, regardless of whether you have half an acre of land or a windowsill. Half of them will accept shade, the other half will forgive you if you forget to water them.

The other four flowers I've chosen here – daffodils, hyacinths, muscari and tulips – are all bulbs and bloom from the end of winter to the end of spring. They can be planted indoors or out for colour when you most need it. You can grow them all and create a riot of colour ready for its Easter card close-up, or just pick one and marvel at how all that plant unfurls from one weird bulb.

All of these flowers will bring you joy throughout several seasons of the year.

DEADHEADING

This chapter is all about flowers, and just as with herbs and vegetables, you want to maximise the plants' productivity. The best way to do this and to keep your plant in bloom is to get rid of its tired-looking flowers – this is known as 'deadheading' and it tricks the plant into thinking it needs to grow more flowers. Sneaky! If you don't remove the tired flowers, the plant will put its energy into producing seeds, and eventually stop blooming.

If the plant's been watered in the past few hours, it's easier to deadhead with just your finger and thumb, because the stems are full of water and will snap more readily. But otherwise take a pair of secateurs, scissors, or even a kitchen knife (I've deadheaded with a grapefruit knife in times of desperation) and just chop off the flower a few centimetres down on its stem.

It's a good idea to pull away yellow, brown or crispy leaves, too. These haven't got enough sunshine. By getting rid of them, the plant will produce new green leaves in their place.

GERANIUMS

Geraniums are not fancy but they possess a kind of simple charm that evokes the laidback vibes of little Mediterranean towns, where they smother window boxes.

They are a popular choice for containers and hanging baskets as they bloom basically anywhere. They are sun worshippers, hailing from South Africa, and will thrive inside on a sunny windowsill, but when growing them outside they will put up with wind, so if in your garden it's a choice between shelter and sun, always choose sun.

There are lots of types of geraniums (technically known as pelargoniums) but the standard sort you'll find in trays in supermarkets and garden centres are called zonal geraniums. They will last the summer months and, if you're lucky, beyond. I've had a geranium flower steadfastly while there has been snow on the ground. Even when I've shoved mine into tin cans and overwatered them in buckets, they still flower forgivingly the next spring.

HOW TO GROW

These are grown most easily from plug plants, and in spring you can barely move for them — supermarkets and nurseries sell them in trays for less than a fiver.

Once you've taken your small plants home, see how well watered they are. If the soil feels dry, give them enough water so that it starts to run through the holes in the bottom of the tray.

You can leave them in the tray for a few days now or get potting immediately. If you like, put a few seedlings into a big pot, as geraniums don't mind sharing space, but make sure they're evenly positioned around the pot with a few centimetres between them.

Make a hole in the soil for the geranium seedling – you can use your hand or a spoon or trowel. Ease the geranium out of the pot and break up the soil around the roots very gently to spread them out a little. Pop the plant into the ground. Fill in around the plant with soil and give it another drink.

Geraniums don't want too much water; a soaking every few days or once a week in summer will do, when the soil at the top of the pot has dried out.

GROWING FROM SEED

If you're feeling keen, or want to try a more unusual kind of geranium, you can grow them from seed. Geranium seeds will grow into plants with flowers in three to four months, so plant them in late winter for summer colour.

Put your seeds on a wet paper towel, fold it up, and put it in a sandwich bag overnight. This dampens the tough outer coatings of the seed and helps them sprout.

Lay out the sprouted seeds carefully on damp soil in little pots or a seedling tray – two or three in each pot or space is about right. Then cover them up with a little extra soil.

Geranium seeds don't need light to start sprouting, but they do like somewhere warm. Give them a delicate sprinkling of water to keep the soil moist.

Once shoots appear, move the seedlings to a sunny windowsill. Lay a clear plastic bag on the windowsill and slide the pots or seedling tray inside it. Let the other side of the bag rest on top: you've created a mini greenhouse!

When the seedlings have grown – they should each have two starter leaves and two 'true' leaves – put them outside to toughen up, or 'harden off'. Start by just putting them out in the mornings and taking them back in before you go to bed, then after a week they're old enough to be left out all night.

HOW TO MAKE THEM LAST

There are a number of ways to make a geranium last for another year – known as 'overwintering' – all of which can seem initially quite confusing.

I keep one pot next to a warm, sheltered wall outside and cut down the watering to once every couple of weeks in the colder seasons. It continues to bloom and grows slightly mad, bendy stems which I thoroughly enjoy.

If you take your plants inside, make sure they have access to light to keep them in bloom.

Be careful not to overwater your geraniums indoors. I moved four into a cramped bucket one winter and they suffered. The soil was sodden and the stems grew mouldy and weak — so go as easy on watering over the winter as if you leave them outside.

If you've kept your plant growing all through the winter, then in the spring cut the stems right back to about 3cm from the base of the plant where it meets the soil. This will encourage bushy growth in the summer.

PROBLEMS

If a geranium's leaves go yellow or a kind of dark reddish brown colour, it isn't getting the right amount of water. Annoyingly, this happens whether they have too much water or not enough. So stick a finger in the soil to test whether it is damp or dry, which should help solve the mystery.

If the soil is too dry, give the plant a bit more water and make sure that you're actually hitting the soil — not just those divine-smelling leaves. If it's too wet, don't panic, just move the pot to a place with plenty of light and don't water it for a week or so.

LAVENDER

Bottle the scent of lavender and you're in old-lady perfume territory, but catch a whiff of the plant fresh on a summer's evening and it can be intoxicating.

Long-stemmed, bushy and with delicate purple buds that let off that aroma, lavender will put up with droughts because it hails from warmer climes. But that hasn't stopped British gardeners from lovingly adopting it.

It looks elegant grown in containers in a smaller garden, inside if it has sufficient drainage, or you can let lavender run riot as a shrub or bush in your garden where it will lure in bees and other insects.

There are dozens of different types, from dwarf varieties to the big and showy, the frilly French versions with blousy flowers or the chic and petite white lavenders. They vary in scent, colour and how long they'll provide you with both, but they generally like similar conditions.

HOW TO BUY

In late spring and early summer it's easy to find lavender plants for sale in supermarkets, nurseries and flower markets. Don't be tempted to go for ones which have loads of flowers on already – this might be their best show of the season. Instead, opt for a plant that has some flower buds, nice, even leafy growth and no white mould around the base. Ask yourself: does this look happy? If it does, that's the one you want.

I've bought overwatered lavender plants before which never had a chance of making it. After planting, their heads will droop and wilt. In some cases, it's easy to accept defeat, rip the plant out and start again. However, before you do this, chop off all the wilted or mouldy growth and make sure the lavender is somewhere with some fresh air blowing around it and lots of sunshine. With some luck, new growth will appear and the plant will survive.

HOW TO GROW

Two really important things to remember with lavender: it loves sunshine and it hates having wet feet (read: roots). So first, pick a sunny spot in your growing space – lavender can handle wind well, too.

If your lavender plants don't have proper drainage or are put in heavy, moisture-rich soil, there's a good chance they will grow tough and woody before just totally giving up. The answer to having loads of beautiful, heady blooms, therefore, is to make sure that you get the soil right before you settle your new plant in.

If you're planting in a container, make sure it has drainage holes, and chuck some crocks – stones, bits of broken-up polystyrene – in there for good measure. Regular potting mix will be fine, but anything that has lots of composted material in will be too rich. You can also mix in a little horticultural grit to your soil, to improve the drainage.

If you're planting lavender straight into your garden and you have quite a heavy soil, mix a little horticultural grit into the planting hole. You can also make a mound out of your flowerbed and plant your lavender into that, this helps the water drain away from the plant, saving its roots from getting waterlogged.

Re-pot the shop-bought plant into your specially prepared soil, and if you're putting a few of them together, make sure they have about 30cm between each plant. They will grow to fill the space.

In the summer, water your lavender regularly and sit back and enjoy watching the bees get involved. Cut back on your watering in winter. If your lavender is in a container, you may want to move it somewhere more sheltered — such as against a wall or under a porch — for the cooler months to stop it getting drowned.

TRIMMING YOUR LAVENDER

Amazing news: it's the end of the summer, and your lavender has survived and grown from strength to strength! Some of the flowers will probably have reached their end by this point, and that's ok, they're meant to.

To make sure your lavender stays bushy and beautiful for next year, it's a good idea to give it a haircut before autumn. This stops its stems from growing brown and tough, or woody. Instead, it will treat you with plenty of fragrant flowers next summer.

Simply cut off the stalks that have flowered and take off about 2–3cm all over the rest of the plant. Make sure you keep some green growth, though. Scoop up your cuttings, pop them in a canvas bag and put it somewhere warm: it will smell divine.

GROWING FROM CUTTINGS

Lavender's not a bad plant to begin your cuttings adventure with, but it does take time to get them going, so you'll want to start in summer so that they are ready for the next spring.

Find a side shoot on an established lavender plant and make sure it's not flowering. Reach down to the bottom of the stem and gently rip it off the plant. This is going to be your cutting.

Strip away the lower leaves, then make a clean cut just above where the cutting ends. Then pinch off the top few leaves. You'll be left with a few leaves and a longer, leaf-free stem. Pinching off the top means that the cutting will put its energy into creating roots, rather than more leaves.

Ideally, you'll want about four cuttings in a flowerpot the size of your palm. Fill the pot with a mix of grit and compost so that the compost is quite gritty, and damp this down a little.

Put your cuttings in against the edge of the pot, placing the leaf-free section into the soil. When their roots grow, they will hit the bottom of the flowerpot, rather than head out of the holes in the bottom. This means they will grow around the pot and form a rootball that can be planted on more quickly.

Put the pot in a light place but not in direct sunlight – this will make the cuttings wilt. Lightly water the pot regularly. You'll have roots growing in about a month.

OSTEOSPERMUM

Osteospermum, otherwise known as African daisy, is just that: a bush of daisies. It comes in a range of colours – from hot pinks and oranges to pale purple – and grows and grows and grows. The word daisy is derived from 'day's eye', which basically means that when the sun comes out the daisies will spread out their petals, then they close when night falls – so don't worry if they look a little sleepy on a gloomy day!

Osteospermum are native to South Africa, so they like it sunny, but they have happily put up with the heavy winds that batter my balcony ledge, where I've perilously grown them for the past couple of summers.

Ideally, they like well-drained sandy soil. but I've plonked them in massive old tomato tins full of compost and they've still bloomed all summer. Osteospermum can either be annual (one-summer) plants, or perennials, which means their growth will slow over winter but they will come back fighting the next year.

These plants don't love frost and cold winters, but osteospermum will survive the winter if you live somewhere fairly mild and they're kept in a sheltered spot, such as against a wall. If they survive the winter, a trim in the new year will give you – and the bees that these plants attract – yet another few months of floral happiness.

HOW TO GROW

There are dozens of varieties of osteospermum available, so you really can take your pick at a flower market, nursery or online – they'll all rub along together quite happily. The easiest time to buy them is in spring and early summer.

Take your pot or tray of plants home and pick a spot that gets some sunlight. Osteospermum will put up with being exposed to wind and shelter equally well, but they do like it bright, so avoid shady spots.

Osteospermum will spread to fill the space they're in, so they're a good choice if you have a patch in a border that looks a bit empty, or some large pots. Either way, make a hole big enough for the plant, tip the plant out of its pot and pop it in the hole. Fill with some potting mix and soil, add in some sand if you're feeling fancy, and throw in some slow-release plant food if you are planting it into a container. Then give it some water.

Although osteospermum aren't especially thirsty plants, they will wilt and look sad if they don't get enough water. Over the summer, if the weather is dry, make sure to top up on your rounds with the watering can. If you're growing it in a container which doesn't have great drainage, go steady to make sure the roots don't rot.

HOW TO PRUNE

As with the other flowers in this chapter, deadheading will lead to fresh blooms on your daisy bush. Just cut off the stem of the tired-looking flower, making sure you don't take off any new buds lower down on the plant.

The one bit of maintenance osteospermum really do thrive off is a good haircut: if they've been flowering since the spring, chopping back the plants in summer will give you more daisies. If your osteospermum is in a container, put it on a table or surface where you can get a good look at it, and cut off the top third of each stem.

It may feel barbaric to chop off flowers and healthy leaves, but you can pop the flowers in a vase inside and use some of the stems as cuttings to make new plants. Ultimately, you'll end up with a neat, bushy daisy plant that will continue flowering until late autumn, rather than a sad, straggly one.

GROWING FROM CUTTINGS

As with lavender, osteospermum are best grown from cuttings. You can take softwood cuttings in spring and early summer by cutting off a bit of the stem that has been newly grown and is still soft, or you can take semi-hardwood cuttings in late summer by cutting off a more mature, woody part of the plant. Both these cuttings can be grown inside over winter so that they are ready to be planted out to bloom the next summer.

Whether you take softwood or semi-hardwood cuttings, the treatment is similar. Get a pot or plastic cup and fill it with potting mix or soil. Make sure there are holes in the bottom of the cup and stick it in a saucer or tray of water. You can either wait for the soil to absorb the water, or water it from the top – it needs to be damp.

Take a cutting about 10cm long from the daisy bush. Strip off the lower leaves and make a neater cut, using a knife, just below a leaf node – the little bump where a new shoot will form. As with lavender, take off any leafy growth on top of the cutting – this will direct the plant's energy into making roots rather than leaves.

You can put a few cuttings in one pot, just make sure that the soil is kept damp and if any cuttings start to rot, remove them. Make sure your pot is somewhere sheltered and relatively warm, and away from direct sunlight. Watch out for roots forming – they should poke out of the bottom in a few weeks.

Once the cuttings are established, you can move them into bigger pots to grow into proper plants. Keep them somewhere warm and bright over winter, before hardening them off outside and moving them into your garden or outdoor space in early spring, where a summer of flowering awaits.

PANSIES

Pansies, in a horticultural sense, are hardcore. They can be grown all year round, but they really thrive over winter and early spring. They will also put up with a lot of crap; they will tolerate cold, wet and windy weather and still put on a good show. Although some will last two years, with a break or 'dormancy period' in between, most are considered one-season plants, or annuals, which means that you'll have to grow them twice if you want them all year round.

But that isn't a big problem if you're a real pansy fan, as the Royal Horticultural Society officially considers them easy enough for children to grow from seed — and, therefore, you can manage it. They come in basically every colour of the rainbow, and you can usually buy them in mixed trays, too.

HOW TO GROW

With the exception of high summer and early autumn, you will be able to find trays of pansies for sale in nurseries and flower markets around the country.

Pansies like good drainage and moist soil and are happy in the sun or with a little shade. The flowerheads follow the light, so if you plant them facing the sun you'll get the best chance of seeing their happy little faces.

Once you've got your starter plants home, gently water them and find a good spot for planting them. Whether in a flowerbed, container or hanging basket, dig a hole the same size as each little pansy and the soil around its roots.

If you're planting into a pot, make sure it has holes in the base. You can also add in some crocks, such as pebbles, or break up the polystyrene tray that the pansies came in and put that at the bottom of the container.

Pop the pansy in its new home and give it another little drink. If it's late autumn, winter or spring, you won't need to do much more than enjoy these plants, as long as they have access to rainwater. Otherwise, check that the soil isn't getting too dry every few days.

Warm temperatures and dry soil can cause pansies to suffer – they'll grow 'leggy' and the flowers will wilt. But you can help them live a little longer if you 'deadhead' faded flowers (see page 82). Simply remove the old flower and the stem it's attached to using a pair of scissors or use your thumb and forefinger to nip it off, to encourage more flower buds. If you manage to do this every few days, or once a week, you'll extend the plant's life.

Pansies are fairly pest-free, but they can attract aphids. The best way to get rid of these is with an insect spray, and there are organic ones available.

GROWING FROM SEED

Pansies grow well from seed and there are countless different colours and varieties available, so it can be helpful to start from scratch if you have a particular colour theme in mind.

However, you do have to play the long game if you choose to sow from seed. If you want pansies in winter, sow in summer. If you want flowers in summer, plant them at the start of the new year.

Either way, the treatment is the same. You can sow your seeds straight outside into the soil, but you might have better luck starting them inside, where the warmer temperatures will help them germinate.

Plant the seeds in a tray of damp potting compost, a centimetre deep and a centimetre apart, or a few to each small pot. Cover them over with soil, then gently water. They should start sprouting in about a week.

When your pansies have six to eight leaves you can move them outside. If there's frost on the ground, you may want to wait until it's a little warmer.

Plant your pansies between 15 and 30cm apart if they're going in a flowerbed, and they will fill the space. They can be a little cosier in a container, but try not to squish too many into a small space.

ONCE PANSIES HAVE FINISHED FLOWERING

With deadheading and good conditions your pansies may last you several months. Eventually, however, they will run out of steam, stop flowering and put out seeds – this is, after all, the pansy's sole life goal.

If you're happy to let nature take its course, leave the pansy be. Its seeds will sow themselves in the ground, the plant will die back, and in a year you may see a whole new plant appearing in the same place.

If you want to plant something else there, that's fine too. Dig up the pansy, chuck it on the compost or in the bin, dig over the soil and start something new.

BULBS

Oak trees from acorns, butterflies from chrysalises: little brown things can create beautiful surprises. Bulbs work in the same way, and the next four flowers all grow from bulbs.

These funny-looking, underwhelming, papery balls go into the earth in the autumn and, months later, just when you've forgotten about them, green shoots will pop up. Discovering the perfect, tiny bloom of a snowdrop when the days are short, grey and cold can feel like witnessing a miracle.

Growing bulbs can get fancy and technical. Experienced gardeners will talk about making 'bulb lasagne' in containers to ensure months of flowers, or cramming dozens into one patch to create a sea of colour. It's impressive, but you can create a different kind of magic by doing something as simple as sticking something in a pot, giving it the occasional water and being patient.

Some bulbs will flower year after year after dying back once they have flowered. If you are planting them in a garden, that's a treat for you to look forward to. If you are a container gardener, I recommend digging them up and starting again in the autumn – soil in containers needs changing every year or so anyway, and it gives you an opportunity to grow something new.

There's a near guarantee that not all the bulbs you plant will sprout or flower. This is normal, and don't worry about it – they're just shy. I'd encourage you to try a couple of different types of bulbs in different places to see how you get on.

If all else fails, you can buy planted bulbs from a florist or nursery, so you can let someone else do the hard work and still get those beautiful spring colours.

SOIL FOR BULBS

Although I've managed to grow flowers from bulbs in containers with poor drainage, they will do better with well-draining, fertile soil. If you have heavy soil, mix in some grit. If you have sandy soil, mix in some compost. There are also special bulb composts available.

FORCING BULBS

If you trick bulbs into thinking they've already gone through winter, you can also make them flower early. This is called forcing, and can be a fun thing to learn how to do if you like having plants and flowers indoors. You can force any of the bulbs in this chapter but muscari or hyacinths are a good place to start.

You'll need to begin forcing bulbs in late summer or early autumn. Fill any container you like – even a pretty ornamental bowl – with damp compost. Put your bulbs, pointy side up, in the container and gently cover with compost, leaving the tops of the bulbs poking out of the soil. Leave enough room so that when you water it won't spill over the edge.

Now your bulbs need to be kept dark and cold. Cover the container completely in a black bag or bin liner to stop light and put them somewhere dark and cold – a garage, shed or shady bit of balcony will do. If you've got the room, use the vegetable drawer of your fridge.

Check back on them every now and then. If the soil is dry, give it a water. When shoots appear out of the soil, the container can be brought indoors. Now the plants need light, but not heat — a windowsill is good, but preferably one that's not near a radiator. You'll see flowers a few weeks afterwards.

LOOKING AFTER BULBS FOR NEXT YEAR

Some gardeners 'lift' their bulbs, which means removing them from the soil and keeping them safe before planting them again later in the year. But at this stage, you can leave your bulbs in the ground to see if they will flower next year.

To give them the best chance, deadhead spent flowers and don't remove any foliage before it turns brown and dies back. This will encourage the bulb to stop putting its energy into making seeds and instead use the remaining green parts of the plant to store up energy for next year's growth.

If you don't like how untidy this looks, you can dig up the bulbs and throw them away, but you'll have to plant new ones again in the autumn for more flowers next year. Remember, though, growing stuff isn't just about things looking pretty all the time — if you let nature do its thing you'll understand your plants and how they work better.

DAFFODILS

The first thing to know about daffodils is that there are lots of different types. Grouped under the term narcissi, there are the big, playful trumpety yellow ones but also the adorable miniature versions, pale pastel-coloured varieties with frilly edges and chic, minimalist paperwhites.

Miniature daffodils, especially those known as tête-à-tête after their pairs of flowers, are as charming as they are cute and are also among the easiest to grow. However, if you buy a bag of general daffodil bulbs from a nursery or, frequently at the end of summer, a supermarket, these will be good, reliable growers, too.

You can buy potted miniature daffodils in flower shops and supermarkets and these can be grown and enjoyed inside or planted outside – they'll pop up again next year.

HOW TO GROW FROM BULBS

Daffodils traditionally herald the coming of spring, and you can expect them to bloom right at the end of winter or just as spring starts, which means their bulbs need planting in the autumn. If you can get hold of the bulbs and are terribly excited, you can get away with planting them in August, but if you forget then they'll still be ok if you plant bulbs into October or November – they'll just bloom later in the new year.

You can grow bulbs in containers or in flowerbeds in the garden. Choose a spot that gets some sun, although daffodils will put up with partial shade.

The daffodil bulbs need to be planted around 10–15cm deep with 5–10cm between them. If you're planting them in a bed, you can either dig up the whole patch where you want to plant the bulbs, lay them down – pointy side up – and then cover up with soil, or use a trowel to dig out little individual holes.

If you are planting them in pots, fill your container until the soil reaches 15cm from the top, lay out your bulbs, pointy side up, then cover with more soil.

Once your bulbs are planted, keep the soil consistently moist but not wet. If your planters don't have access to rainwater, you'll need to keep them watered until the winter.

HOW TO GROW FROM A PLANT / ONCE THE BULBS HAVE SPROUTED

In February and March you'll be able to buy sprouting daffodils in pots – but choose one that hasn't properly bloomed yet. Look out for the little green buds at the end of the stems, as these will turn into flowers.

If you're growing your plant indoors, find a spot that gets as much natural light as possible. There's no need to re-pot if you're growing indoors, just pop the plastic pot on a saucer or in a more decorative pot. Check the soil – it should feel moist. If it doesn't, give it some water. Wait, and you'll be surprised by sweet little flowers sooner than you think!

If you're moving the daffodil straight into soil, find a spot that's not too shady and dig a hole the same size as the pot. Water the soil before you put your plant in, pop it in, and then water it again.

Daffodils can flower better if they get some fertiliser in early spring. Some liquid tomato feed will do the trick.

Although daffodils do benefit from deadheading, the extra energy that this encourages the plant to put into flowering is saved up for next year's flowers, so don't expect more flowers from the same stem in one season.

ONCE DAFFODILS HAVE FINISHED FLOWERING

This is the point when you need to work out whether you want to have daffodils again next year, and suffer the plant looking a little ugly for a few weeks, or kick it out and start something else growing in that spot.

Daffodil bulbs get their energy to flower again the following year from their leaves. If you cut them back before every leaf has gone brown and died back, you're limiting the chance of having flowers from the same bulbs next year. Once all the foliage has died back, you can cut it off.

HYACINTHS

Heavy with a rich, heady perfume and tubular mounds of tiny little flowers, hyacinths are a full-on flower. They come in a variety of colours, but I love growing the white ones inside in a large glass container on a bed of moss, which allows me to admire their tangle of roots beneath the big show above.

Hyacinths are easy to grow from bulbs. In the wild in Syria, where they originate from, they grow in the bright light and cool ground and bloom in the spring, and they do similar things if you plant them outside in the UK. But people have learned to 'force' hyacinths indoors to grow and bloom in a matter of weeks – traditionally in time for Christmas.

You can buy ready planted forced hyacinths from late autumn through to early spring which will fill your home with scent and colour, or try to grow bulbs that have been especially grown for blooming inside in the middle of winter. If you have sensitive skin, wear a pair of gloves, as the papery surface of the bulbs can cause irritation.

HOW TO GROW

Hyacinths are easy to grow and, if grown directly in the soil in the right spot, will come back year after year. You'll want to get cracking in the autumn. Choose somewhere that gets plenty of light and with good, well-draining soil – you may want to mix in some compost with your soil – and plant each bulb 10cm deep.

Hyacinths get lonely and will flower much better if you plant them in a triangle of three than by themselves, so if you have the space, place three bulbs about 8cm away from each other.

If the soil is moist, you shouldn't need to add any extra water to bed them in. If not, water it a little.

They also grow really well in containers, although they are at a greater risk of frost damage there than in the ground. Fill your container with potting mix or John Innes No 2 and dampen down the soil. Plant the bulbs 10cm deep and 5cm apart: hyacinth bulbs can get a little friendlier with each other in a pot and will create a more impressive display with lots of bulbs in one place. Make sure the soil stays moist, but not wet, over winter.

Whether in the ground or a container, you can expect to see green shoots by the new year and flowers in early spring.

HOW TO GET HYACINTHS FLOWERING BY CHRISTMAS

In the run up to Christmas, when the days are short and indulgence of all kinds is running high, there is something pleasing about the crisp, clean sight of spring flowers emerging from a bowl. Forcing hyacinths involves a bit of maths to get them flowering on time, but it's not that complicated once you've planted the bulbs. If nothing else, your mum will be incredibly proud of you.

Head to a garden centre or nursery from September and there will be a range of bulbs, hopefully with some indication on their packaging as to how many weeks they take to bloom. Pick the type you fancy and which will fit with your timeframe.

Choose a container and put a layer of damp compost in the bottom. Put the bulbs, pointy side up, on the compost. Make sure they don't touch each other or the side of the container, but keep them close together. Cover with compost and leave room at the top to water. If you want to decrease the light levels further, you can put the container in a black bin bag.

Move the container to a dark place and check every week for shoots. When they appear, move the pot somewhere with plenty of room, and take off the bag.

Water only when the soil is dry. You should have flowers within three weeks. Happy Christmas!

ONCE HYACINTHS HAVE FINISHED FLOWERING

When hyacinths have bloomed fully, their flowers will fade, crisp up and turn brown and their stems may start to bend over. At this point, take some scissors or secateurs and deadhead just below where the flower head starts. This will keep the plant tidy and attractive until the other stems have stopped blooming.

If you're growing hyacinths outside, let them die back naturally. You can tidy up the foliage once it has all turned brown. If you've forced your bulbs, they are unlikely to bloom as well next year, so appreciate what you had and throw the bulbs away once they have flowered.

MUSCARI

To my mind, muscari, or grape hyacinths, could be something mythical creatures would dance around. They're frequently blue, although you can get white ones, and look like a tiny bunch of grapes (hence the alternative name) suspended upside down on a green stick. After a mass of long, floppy green leaves, the first sign you'll get of the incoming muscari-fest in spring is seeing little pale blue bumps poking out of the cold soil.

Their vivid blue heads can last a few delightful weeks in the spring and I love the strange, bulbous green seed pods that the flowers leave in their wake and which hang about until you get around to doing some late-spring planting.

As a container gardener, I don't suffer from this problem, but it's worth bearing in mind that muscari can spread if you plant it in your garden.

Because they are small, muscari's pastel-hued blooms can look stylish when it's grown indoors – it can look just plain adorable planted in a teacup with some moss. Muscari can also be forced to bloom earlier than spring if you just can't wait.

HOW TO GROW FROM BULBS

Muscari bulbs like their soil well-drained, and a bit of mixed-in compost won't hurt whether you're planting straight into the garden or in containers.

Muscari are very tolerant and will handle full sun or partial shade. Their diminutive height makes them a perfect flower to grow underneath or around bigger plants or shrubs or along a border.

I've squished loads of muscari bulbs in together in containers and they've grown happily enough, but do plant them 10cm below the soil surface.

HOW TO MAKE THEM FLOWER OVER WINTER INDOORS

To get muscari flowering early, otherwise known as forcing, you'll need to start planting in late summer or at the very beginning of autumn.

Find a container that is at least 10cm deep and, if you want to grow a few flowers, the same width. Muscari grow long, floppy stems, so a high-sided glass container will stop them from falling over.

Fill your pot with damp potting soil and keep a 3–5cm gap between the top of the container and the top of the soil.

You can pack your muscari bulbs in pretty closely, and this will make for an impressive show when they flower. Aim to plant 10–12 in a container that's about the size of a postcard. Then cover them up in a black or paper bag, and put them somewhere cold and ideally dark for eight weeks.

Check your bulbs every couple of weeks for green shoots. You can also dampen down the soil if it's dry. When green shoots appear, take the muscari out of the dark and put them somewhere bright but not too warm.

Water them every few days and watch out for those little blue heads popping up.

HOW TO GROW FROM PLANTED BULBS

If you've fallen in love with some muscari that have already been planted up, you can take them home to grow indoors or plant outdoors. With any luck, they'll come back again next year.

Pick a plant that isn't yet in full flower – some of the buds should be pale or maybe still tucked partially into the soil.

If you're keeping your new muscari indoors, there's no need to re-pot it. Perhaps put it on a saucer or in a prettier pot, and if the soil is dry, give it a light watering every few days.

If you want to plant your muscari outside, find a good spot. If it's winter, there's a good chance the soil will be damp, but if it's not, water the earth and dig a hole big enough for your bulbs. You can separate the different muscari stalks and place them around your growing space – just tease each bulb apart gently.

Put the muscari bulbs and their surrounding soil in the hole, pat down and give it a light water. After that, they won't need much attention unless they don't have access to rainwater.

ONCE MUSCARI HAVE FINISHED FLOWERING

I personally enjoy the green seedheads that emerge after muscari have finished flowering so much that I don't trim the flowers after they are past their best. Muscari also last well as a cut flower, so I sometimes chop them down to the stem to display in the home, too. However, deadheading the flowers encourages a better show the year after, it's your choice, really.

If you just leave them well alone, muscari take a while to die back. For several weeks after they've flowered, they will put out seedheads and those green stems will stay green and lush. After about six weeks the leaves will turn yellow, and this is when you can cut them back. Once the stem has turned green, you can cut this down to the soil too.

If you are an impatient container gardener like me, you may want to change things up for late spring. If so, use a trowel or spoon to dig out the bulb – just follow the stem of the muscari under the surface of the soil, and pull it out.

TULIPS

I've grown tulips for a couple of springs now, and each time those triumphantly regal blooms appear out on the balcony I'm astonished that they've grown there. Tulips are the kind of flower you pick up for a fiver, so to come home from a long day to find them quietly blooming in a plastic flowerpot is a genuine marvel.

They are, however, easy to grow and can look just fabulous emerging out of a flowerbed or trumpeting around in a pot. Tulips come in every colour under the sun and I've grown the sleekly elegant and ludicrously frilly varieties with equal success, too.

They're also real chameleons: parrot tulips that start off a rather hideous pale yellow and bright red will transform to sumptuous raspberry-ripple wonders within a week, while bright pink varieties will mature to a deep red before their days are done.

I'd advise you to try a few different types, or perhaps buy a mixed bag of bulbs. I'm all for minimalism in colour schemes, but try not to be disappointed if you don't manage to grow a tub of perfectly level, simultaneously blooming flowers – this is the stuff of witchcraft.

Instead, plant your tulip bulbs, keep a watchful eye on them and be prepared for a marvel: whatever appears, it will be a wonder.

HOW TO GROW FROM BULBS

Tulips are among the last bulbs to flower – you can expect to see them bloom anywhere between March and May – and as a result they're some of the last to be planted, too. You'll need to put them in the ground in October or November, when the roots will form best in the colder temperatures.

Tulips like full sun and hate being overly wet, which is worth bearing in mind before you plant your bulbs. They're not meant to love wind but mine battled gales last spring just fine.

Different varieties of bulbs will need to be planted at different depths, so check the back of the packet for the specifics. But generally, tulip bulbs need to be planted 15cm deep and between 8 and 12cm apart, especially if you're planting them in your garden.

Dig a hole 15–20cm deep and arrange your tulip bulb with the pointed end facing upwards. Cover the hole with soil, pat down and water.

If you're planting tulips in a container you can move the bulbs closer together, but make sure they don't touch as this can encourage disease to spread. More bulbs in your container will result in a more impressive show once they bloom.

Although they do need water to grow, tulips can rot if they get too wet so don't be tempted to water them too vigorously over winter. If they get access to rainwater they'll be fine, and if they don't get rained on then a regular splash on your rounds will suffice – about once a week or so. The soil should never feel wet to the touch. Keep your watering consistent when the first shoots start to appear.

HOW TO GROW FROM PLANTS

You may find planted tulip bulbs sprouting and ready to go into your garden at nurseries and flower markets in spring. Some of these will have been forced, and are suitable for growing and enjoying indoors, others can go straight into the garden.

If you're growing your tulip indoors, make sure it gets plenty of access to light and only water it when the soil feels dry to the touch.

If you want to brighten up your garden, check the soil of your new tulips before you plant them in the ground. It should be moist – water it if it's not.

Find somewhere sheltered and sunny. Dig a hole that's the same size as the pot and shake the tulips free of their pot before planting them in the hole. Pat down and give them a little more water.

ONCE TULIPS HAVE FINISHED FLOWERING

Tulip flowers can last for a week or two, so don't be too hasty to act until they've completely finished flowering. When they are, their petals will start to fall off.

If you have an abundance of tulips they make lovely cut flowers for the home, especially when they've flowered for a few days outside. Cut them off at the bottom of the stem – if you carefully prick them directly beneath the head of the flower with a pin, they won't droop as readily when kept in water.

While some tulips will return for another year, most people replace bulbs the following autumn for the best flowers. If you want to keep yours, deadhead the flowers once the petals start to fall, but keep the stem.

...minator, the world's most famous tech incubator, leading to a sale to Twitter and a plush job at Facebook. In *Chaos Monkeys*, he attempts a tell-all memoir about a technology industry that inspires both awe and fear across the globe.

The memoir gets its title from a software concept. Garcia Martinez describes "computer systems. Garcia Martinez's memoir are people that are fool that trepreneurs they are society's cha-monkeys, pulling the plug or radi-onal industries. The book's US subtitle 'Obscene Fortune and Random Fail-? in Silicon Valley" — reinforces the a that this chaos-making is not 'ays justifiable.

arcia Martinez can be funny and his

of high-powered Californians: "Th won't hold it against you if you're a right over a homeless person on the way to a mindfulness yoga class."

...s for example, 1 ...s venture cap... as "the fin ...doubt of individuals w... "discipline and ambition but no actual tale...

The memoir's major fla... Garcia Martinez never makes... read feel that he is the likeable grown-up the Silicon Valley theme park; h appears just as out of touch and juvenile as his colleagues. In particular, in ar

4

HOUSEPLANTS

If you don't have a garden, a balcony or even a window box, then prepare to fall in love with houseplants. Plenty of people adore them even if they do have some outdoor space, because there are masses of houseplants to choose from – from massive, tumbling vines to the tiniest miniature cactus – and they can be some of the most relaxed plants around.

The best will forgive you when you go on holiday for a week and forget to water them, then surprise you by putting out an outrageous bloom every few months. Oxalis, which is included in this chapter, can be filed under that category.

Maidenhair ferns, by contrast, can be quite demanding, but they are so fascinating and beautiful that they'll made an adoring plant parent out of anyone, so they're included here, too.

Houseplant aficionados will create miniature jungles in their homes, with whole bathtubs filled up on a dedicated watering day. Other people may just take pleasure in one particularly good plant.

Whichever you turn out to be, understanding how much water, light and space houseplants need is essential – after that, they'll grow steadily, filling you with wonder along the way.

SUCCULENTS

Succulents have experienced somewhat of a renaissance in recent years. They usually come in shades of pale green, aqua-blue and even purple and have squishy-looking leaves which are filled with sap to keep the plant alive when they're in their naturally dry habitat.

As most homes aren't deserts, succulents tend to come in small pots, ready to perk up a shelf or windowsill. But while succulents can be very easy to look after, beginners don't always know exactly what the plants need.

In essence, succulents like it dry and warm. Too little sunlight will cause them to grow tall and leggy — otherwise known as etiolation — with fewer leaves. Some people really like this, I'm one of them, but the plant won't grow in the way you might imagine it.

Too much direct sunlight, however, can cause a succulent's leaves to be scorched and change colour. Again, I keep some succulents on a sunny windowsill and simply accept that in the summer they will turn dark red. They return to green once autumn arrives.

It's water, however, that can be a succulent killer. They can handle a drought but if you give them too much to drink you'll end up with a mouldy dead plant on your hands. Thankfully, there's a simple way to see if your succulent needs watering: check its leaves. If they are wrinkly and shrivelled, it's time to water — use a spray mister in the middle of the plant, if you have one. If you don't, gently pour in some water from a bottle. If they are plump and shiny, you can leave it for a few more days.

Succulents are really easy to propagate, to make new plants from the old ones. They are grown almost entirely from cuttings, but they skip a step that most plants need – the human involvement of cutting off a bit – by simply sprouting new little buds and leaves which grow roots and plant themselves.

There are two succulents included in this chapter: aloe vera, the friendliest beginner succulent around, and a money tree. Both are highly tolerant, stylish and easy to propagate. Consider them the first step in your succulent education.

ALOE VERA

Aloe vera is known in some circles for its supposedly miraculous beauty and medicinal benefits. I don't know much about those, although I have snapped a long, spiny leaf off one of my aloe vera plants and liberally applied the goo inside to a friend's sunburn, which brought her some relief.

What I do know about aloe vera is that it will bring to your growing armoury a plant that is high in tolerance, low on maintenance and has tiny little teeth. And who doesn't want a plant with teeth?

Aloe originates from around the Sahara Desert, but it has been grown around the world for centuries because it will put up with non-desert conditions – such as your bathroom.

HOW TO GROW

Aloe vera can be found readily in flower shops and some nurseries, and you'll probably be able to pick one up for a song.

It's worth keeping it in its pot at first, as aloe veras can live in small pots quite happily. However, if it is so overgrown that it is toppling over, it's time to move on. Find a pot only slightly larger than the one it came in, and move it over with as much of the original soil as possible. Make up the rest of the room with potting soil.

Aloe vera can put up with less light than some succulents, but it will still need to be somewhere bright or near a window. If it doesn't have enough light, its leaves will lie flat, rather than stick upwards happily. If you expose it to too much sunlight, this can turn its leaves a dull brown colour and can eventually burn them.

Take a look at your aloe vera's leaves. Are they plump and slightly bouncy to the touch? In which case, you don't need to water it. If, however, the leaves are thin and floppy, give it a small drink. Keep an eye on the plant – by the next day it should have absorbed that water into its leaves and they will have plumped up. If they haven't, give it some more water.

In the summer, you can soak the aloe vera's soil and it will be alright – just make sure that you let the soil dry out in between watering.

KEEPING YOUR ALOE VERA LOOKING GOOD

As time goes on, some of your aloe vera's leaves may turn crispy and brown. This could be because they are sunburned. If so, move your plant to a place with less direct sunshine – away from a window or next to one with frosted glass – and cut off the damaged leaf at its base on the stem with a sharp knife. Give it a big drink to recover.

If your aloe vera's leaves are going brown but mushy, this suggests it's being overwatered and is going mouldy. Cut right back on your watering and wait for the soil to dry out. If the leaves are still mouldy, cut them back to the stem to save the rest of the plant.

RE-POTTING ALOE VERAS

I never fail to be amazed by how tightly bound aloe vera roots can get. They will put up with a tiny amount of space. When, however, your plants are falling over with tedious regularity, it's time to give them an upgrade.

While most plants are generally happy in a good all-round soil, succulents really do benefit from a succulent potting mix. It recreates the sandy, well-draining soil that they grow best in, and it is worth spending a few quid on a bag at the garden centre if you want to propagate lots of succulents.

Get a pot that is only a little bigger than the one your aloe vera currently inhabits and make sure it has a hole in the bottom. If the aloe vera doesn't have drainage, it will rot.

If you've got some grit or gravel to hand, put this in the bottom of the pot, otherwise just tip in your succulent potting mix. If you're not using succulent mix, try to add some sand or grit to your usual potting mix.

Leave a hole in the new pot that's the same size as the one your aloe vera is currently in. Place your hand over where the plant and the soil meet (mind those teeth) and turn the whole lot upside down over the new pot. Then place the rootball in the soil. Pat down.

Unlike potting up flowers, vegetables or herbs, succulents benefit from a couple of dry days in their new homes before being watered.

MAKING NEW ALOE VERA PLANTS

If you wait long enough, your aloe vera plant will grow a tiny version of itself, known as an offshoot or a pup, near its stem. This is a new baby plant that can be grown by itself.

Gently pull on the baby plant and it should easily come free of the bigger one. It will have a couple of short roots attached. Plant this in a small pot of soil, ideally succulent mix. Wait a day or so, and water.

If your aloe vera hasn't put out any pups, you can still propagate from leaves. Take a knife and cut off a healthy looking leaf. Put it to the side somewhere dry and cool for a week or two, and let that juicy cut scab over.

Once it has dried up, dip it in honey (you may want to use a spoon, rather than stick the leaf into your entire jar) – this acts as a natural preventative against mould or bugs. Let the honey run off, then stick your cutting cut-side down in a pot of succulent mix. Here it should root within a few weeks.

A ... Valley success: a start-up in Y-Combinator, the world's most famous tech incubator, leading to a sale to Twitter and a plush job at Facebook. In *Chaos Monkeys*, he attempts a tell-all memoir about a technology industry that inspires both awe and fear across the globe.

The memoir gets its title from a soft-ware tool that ... ience of computer systems. García Martínez d... entrepreneurs: they are society's cha... monkeys, pulling the plug or tradi-tional industries. The book's US subtitle — "Obscene Fortune and Random Fail-ure in Silicon Valley" — reinforces the idea that this chaos-making is not always justifiable.

García Martínez can be funny and his book feels darkly true. Facebook employees, he suggests, are as devoted

of high-powered Californians: "They won't hold it against you if you're a no-show at their wedding and they'll step right over a homeless person on their way to a mindfulness yoga class." At fi... ... s venture cap... ...ggressive ... for example, he ... as "the final res... redoubt of individuals w... discipline and ambition but no actual tale..."

The memoir's major flav... is ... list García Martínez never makes ... reader feel that he is the likeable gr... in the Silicon Valley theme park: he appears just as out of touch and juvenile as his colleagues. In particular, in an industry that has struggled to welcome women, he does little to hide his sexism

INSIDE THE SILICON VALLEY
MONEY MACHINE
Antonio García Martínez

Harper $29.99
528 pages

MONEY TREE

My grandfather had an enormous money tree that thrived on neglect.
It sat in a huge brass bowl, was very rarely watered and gave forth so
many baby money trees that I have both a great-grandbaby money tree
and its nephew in the same room of my flat.

They're not enormously sexy as succulents go, but I have a soft spot
for their fat, shiny leaves. Also known as a jade tree, friendship tree or
lucky tree, the Crassula ovata looks like a cartoon tree and is essentially
unkillable as long as it is kept dry. Although money trees can be
found growing all over the world, they are native to South Africa and
Mozambique, so they are drought-tolerant.

If you're venturing into the world of succulents for the first time, a
money tree is a good way to launch a potential obsession with these
houseplant favourites. They're easy to get hold of, usually very cheap
and, once rooted, grow quite quickly, although they may take a couple of
decades to get to their full height of around a metre tall.

Best of all, even an inexpert eye can usually work out what's going on
with them with just a cursory glance.

HOW TO GROW

You can pick up small money trees in most garden centres and
supermarkets all year round — just head to their houseplant section.
They're generally very affordable, a small one shouldn't cost much
more than a fiver.

Take your new money tree home and, if you're feeling fancy, pop it in a decorative pot. It's highly unlikely to need re-potting, money trees can stay in the same pot for a few years.

Put it somewhere with good access to natural light, but be aware that direct sunlight will cause the leaves to change colour and even be scorched. A shelf in a light room may be better than a windowsill.

The best way to tell if a money tree needs watering is to look at its leaves: when they are shiny and fat, the money tree doesn't need to be watered. If the leaves are shrivelled or wrinkled, it needs a drink. Give it enough water so it runs out of the bottom of the pot, then leave it be until the leaves wrinkle again – probably in about a week's time. It will need less watering in winter.

If you like, give it some liquid fertiliser every few weeks during spring and summer, but your money tree will be just fine without.

HOW TO GROW FROM SCRATCH

Like most succulents, money trees can be a doddle to propagate. In the wild, they are possibly the world's most casual reproducers: they can spread new life by simply standing there and letting their branches drop off. These branches grow roots and then go forth and conquer.

You can grow money trees from seed, and there are plenty of kits out there that will give you the equipment to do this. However, if you've got a friend with a money tree, or if you've got a shop-bought one and want to make some friends with new money trees, you can make a new one from the existing plant.

Find a good, healthy looking branch and use a clean, sharp knife to cut it off from the main stem. Your cutting should be about 10cm long.

Remove some of the leaves from the lower part of the cutting and put the cutting in a small glass of water. If you put sellotape across the top of the glass, this will stop the branch falling into the water or out of the glass. Roots should appear in about 10 days to two weeks. When they have, you can plant the cutting in a pot of soil – ideally some succulent or cactus mix, but otherwise normal potting mix will do.

Gently water it at first, and put in a bright place. In time, your cutting will grow more leaves and branches.

MAIDENHAIR FERN

Maidenhair ferns are as beautiful as their name would attest. They can also be as princessy. The price to pay for those tumbling fronds of delicate, scalloped leaves is consistent and dedicated care: but once you know where to put your fern and how to keep it happy, it will reward you every few days with tiny little green stalks which unfurl in a way that is both amazing and adorable. It's worth it.

In the wild, maidenhair ferns grow in damp, shady places such as waterfalls and rock walls, and some gardeners manage to make them thrive as part of a fern wall outside. But pretty much anyone can keep one alive as a houseplant in the right conditions. In fact, they are quite resilient: even the most defeated-looking maidenhair fern can put out new leaves with a good water and some time.

Things maidenhair ferns don't like include draughts, bright light, cigarette smoke, gas fumes, dry soil and standing in water. Things they like the best are consistently moist soil. Remember that, and you'll be fine.

HOW TO GROW

Depending on where you live, you may struggle to find a maidenhair fern in your local nursery all year round, so have a chat with the staff there to find out when they may get one in and keep your eyes out or try a local florist or specialist plant shop. You can also find them easily online.

Once you've got your maidenhair fern home, don't be tempted to re-pot it straight away. It will probably have been planted in the right soil, and they like compact pots, so moving it into a bigger home may upset it.

Instead, think carefully about where to put it. I initially kept my maidenhair fern in a dark, draughty hallway and let it sit with its roots in standing water for a week, which is a recipe for death. Miraculously, I didn't kill it before I moved it to a shelf in my bathroom. Now it gets misted every time someone uses the shower, and gets a small amount of filtered light from the window. Bathrooms are a good home for maidenhair ferns because they recreate the damp conditions they enjoy and often have misted windows, so they won't get scorched by sunlight.

Once your maidenhair fern is in place, check the soil. It should feel damp. If it doesn't, water the soil and, even better, use a mister or spray bottle to gently wet the leaves. Putting the pot on a tray or saucer with pebbles and water in will help keep the roots moist, but letting it stand in water will lead them to rot and the plant could die.

Lightly spraying the leaves every couple of days, especially if the room doesn't get condensated normally, will stop them from going brown and encourage them to grow. In the spring and summer, adding some liquid fertiliser to the water once a month will help guarantee success.

HOW TO KEEP IT LOOKING NICE

It's totally normal for a maidenhair fern's leaves to dry out or go brown and, frankly, a little manky, even if you have been misting like a dedicated fern parent. Princess maidenhair fern doesn't like having brown leaves, so chop off the entire frond at the base of the stem: others will grow in its place.

If just a few leaves are brown, you can cut these off at the base of their individual stem where they join the others.

Even if you end up giving your fern quite a drastic haircut, that's ok: soon enough more leaves will grow to fill their place.

HOW TO GET MORE FERNS

Ferns don't grow from seed but via spores which appear on the underside of their leaves. In spring and summer you'll see these like little fingernails on your plant's leaves.

It is possible to grow new ferns from these, but it's a fairly technical process and takes at least three to four months to see any results. Instead, if you want new ferns, it's a better bet to divide the rootball of an established fern into smaller pieces and plant these up as separate plants.

It's best to do this in the spring. You can put the newly separated root clumps into regular potting mix, but adding in some compost or leaf mould will help it along.

OXALIS

The tiny, compact houses of Tokyo don't have front gardens. Instead, clustered around the front doors are pots, many of which are filled with the appropriately geometric purple leaves of oxalis, otherwise known as purple shamrock.

There's something rather lovely about these deep purple, triangular leaves. I've grown both the green-and-purple, round-edged varieties and the purple in the warm, sheltered parts of my balcony, but both thrive indoors, too, and cut a stylish dash as a houseplant.

Oxalis will come and go from tiny little bulbs. When they're not happy, their spindly stems will die back, but keep the soil relatively moist and fuzzy new shoots will spring up. They will send up delicate pale pink flowers every few months when the conditions are right.

HOW TO GROW

In certain types of artfully designed florists and home shops, you might see oxalis for sale, often in a hand-thrown ceramic pot, for a hefty price tag. I prefer to pick mine up from flower markets or nurseries, where they normally cost less than a fiver. But they can be hard to track down, so if you can justify the cost, treat yourself.

Oxalis are tolerant but they like nice, bright light. That doesn't have to be a windowsill, especially as direct sunlight can scorch the leaves, but basically nowhere too dingy. Oxalis turn to face the light, so you will want to turn an established plant around to make sure it doesn't just grow in one direction.

You probably won't need to re-pot your oxalis straight away. In fact, it can sit tight until it looks like it's bursting out of its pot, but this can happen quite quickly if the plant is happy. Make sure that whatever you're potting it into has drainage, as they don't like being overly damp.

Oxalis will survive an irregular watering pattern, but if it gets too dry then it will retreat into its bulb under the soil. Similarly, if it gets too wet, you won't have much luck. Instead, give it a good soaking and, unless it's been incredibly hot, wait a few days to a week to check the soil. When the top of the soil feels dry, give it another big drink.

HOW TO GROW FROM BULBS

I planted some oxalis bulbs in mid-autumn one year, fully expecting them not to appear for six months. Within a few weeks they were putting out stems and leaves, even blooming a couple of days before Christmas — and all of this was outside.

In short: in the right conditions, oxalis are incredibly easy to grow from bulbs. While most bulbs prefer to be spread out, oxalis are pretty happy in their own company: you can squidge half a dozen in a pot that's about 20cm wide.

Put some soil in the pot and firm it down. Stick your finger or the end of a pencil or paintbrush into the soil about 2–3cm deep. Make your holes about 6–8cm apart. Pop the oxalis bulbs into the hole – any way around will do, they will grow regardless. Water the soil and keep it moist, but not wet. You should see shoots popping up in two to three weeks.

WHEN OXALIS GETS LANKY

If oxalis doesn't have the treatment it likes it will grow long, droopy stems and stunted leaves. This might be because it didn't get the right amount of water – either too much, or not enough – or it is straining for more light.

Here you've got two options: try to save it by improving your watering routine and moving it into a brighter spot, or accept defeat and force the plant into dormancy. This is the better option for lazy/busy gardeners: simply stop watering the oxalis as much. Your oxalis will die back and, if you move it into a brighter spot, come back in a few weeks' time fighting.

Don't be tempted to chop off or pull out the ugly, weakened stems. I know they don't look great, but they are still photosynthesising and giving energy to the bulb so it can pull off an ugly duckling act later. If you really can't bear to look at it, move the oxalis somewhere bright but tucked away, maybe on a shelf or in the bathroom.

WHEN YOU WANT MORE OXALIS

If it's happy, oxalis grows fast. This can make it a pest in some gardens, where it spreads across flowerbeds, but in the home, that simply means more plants to give away to friends.

It's a simple plant to propagate, or make new plants from. When your oxalis is established, look to where the stems meet the soil – you should see a few of them emerging from the same spot. Give this a gentle tug and a lift, and you'll bring the bulb up from the soil. Try your best to bring out any root growth at the same time.

This clump can then be divided: it'll be quite obvious where you can pull the separate bits of clump apart, so do this gently. Now plant up those little parts of the clump into their own smaller pots. Bingo: new oxalis plants, ready to go.

GARDENING TERMS EXPLAINED

Annual: A plant that will grow from seed, flower, put out seeds and die all in the space of one year or growing season.

Biennial: A plant that will grow from seed in the first year, then flower, put out seeds and die in its second year or growing season.

Bolting: When a plant chooses to grow seeds, rather than leaves, because the temperature of its soil has risen very suddenly. You want to stop edible plants from doing this.

Crocks: Objects that improve the drainage in a container by increasing the flow of water out of a container and stopping soil from getting waterlogged. These can be bits of broken flowerpot, polystyrene plant trays or stones.

Cutting: A piece of an established plant that is removed and re-potted in order to grow another plant.

Deadheading: The process of removing older flowers to prevent the plant making seeds and to encourage it to spend more energy on new flowers or harvesting energy to bloom again next year.

Germination: The term used to describe when a seed has started growing, and will put out shoots.

Growbag: A makeshift container or purpose-made plastic bag, sometimes filled with compost and fertiliser, that offers the room to grow vegetables in.

Hardening off: When a seedling or plant that has been grown inside gets accustomed to the conditions outside over a short period of time.

Leggy: The term given to plants that have grown tall and spindly due to a lack of light or nourishment. Plants that are reaching the end of their flowering season can also become leggy.

Overwintering: Helping a plant to survive the colder seasons to grow and bloom again the next year.

Patting down: Firming down the soil around a rootball of a plant once it has been moved from its original pot into the ground or a larger container.

Perennial: A plant that will put out one flush of flowers, die back over the winter and then return the next year to flower again.

Pinching out: Encouraging fuller, stronger growth by snapping off the top part of a particularly tall seedling above two leaf nodules.

Pollination: When pollen from the male part of a plant is transferred to a female part of a plant in order to fertilise it and make seeds.

Pot-bound: When a plant has grown too large for its current container and may be suffering as a result.

Potting on: Moving a plant into a larger container to improve its growth.

Propagating: Growing new plants from those you already have through cuttings or seeds.

Self-seeding: When a plant is able to distribute its own seeds after flowering – most often annuals and biennials at the end of their life cycle – encouraging more plants of the same type to grow around it.

Thinning out: The act of removing smaller or weaker seedlings or small plants in order to let the larger, healthier plants thrive.

True leaves and starter leaves: The first two leaves a seedling will put out are called starter leaves. True leaves appear next, and it's these that should be counted to judge the growth of a plant and whether it's ready to be moved on.

Truss: A cluster of smaller stems from a main branch where tomatoes will start to grow.

INDEX